WHAT OTHERS ARE SAYING

"Kevin is the original. He demystifies the pre-sales process and makes it easy for any builder to boost profits and create momentum in new community launches far beyond where they typically would be. It isn't theory, but something he did as builder himself that was created out of necessity during the Great Recession that has immense value in any market."

Mike Lyon
Do You Convert

"Kevin is a gem in the homebuilding industry—he really 'gets' marketing, people, and technology. Then he combines all those elements into processes that consistently work!"

Dave Clements
CEO of Lasso CRM

"No one is more provocative or passionate about marketing new homes than Kevin Oakley. ... Kevin has captured a simple formula that he manages to teach in a remarkably enchanting way. Learn the lessons, and you'll become a more successful marketer."

Myers Barnes, MIRM
Myers Barnes Associates, Inc.

Be a unicorn!

PRESALE WITHOUT FAIL

THE SECRET TO LAUNCHING NEW COMMUNITIES WITH MAXIMUM RESULTS

KEVIN OAKLEY

Publisher: **Corey Michael Blake**
President: **Kristin Westberg**
Editor: **Carly Cohen**
Creative Director: **Sunny DiMartino**
Cover Design: **Analee Paz**
Interior Design: **Christy Bui**
Project Manager: **Leeann Sanders**
Proofreaders: **Adam Lawrence, Sunny DiMartino**

© 2018 Kevin Oakley

Writers of the Round Table Press
PO Box 1603, Deerfield, IL 60015
www.roundtablecompanies.com

Printed in the United States of America

First Edition: September 2018
10 9 8 7 6 5 4 3 2 1

Library of Congress Cataloging-in-Publication Data
Oakley, Kevin.
Presale without fail: the secret to launching
new communities with maximum results /
Kevin Oakley.—1st ed. p. cm.
ISBN Paperback: 978-1-61066-071-6
ISBN Digital: 978-1-61066-072-3
Library of Congress Control Number: 2018955090

Writers of the Round Table Press and the logo
are trademarks of Writers of the Round Table, Inc.

Melanie, Avery, Sydney, Hayden, and Mason
*Thank you for the unending love and support
you show me—even when Daddy has to be on the road. I want
to make a positive impact on others, but none more than you.*

Marty Gillespie
*Thank you for giving me the opportunity to
"let loose" on your company while at Heartland Homes.
Without that freedom this book would not exist.*

CONTENTS

BACKGROUND AND OVERVIEW

WHY I WROTE THIS BOOK

The PreSale Without Fail (PSWF) program was created for a single purpose—to create more profitable sales for home builders and developers. More specifically, PSWF is about launching new communities and phases correctly to create more sales, and the momentum to carry the project through to the final sale.

Over twelve years of hard work and intense study have gone into the development of this program—and it has proven itself again and again. It has resulted in anywhere from eight to fifty homes sold in a single day. It has worked in locations with high demand, and locations where pent-up demand is non-existent. It has worked with great sales teams and good ones. It is not dependent on model homes, finished home sites, or even paved streets.

I've included a step-by-step outline of the process, and you're welcome to skip ahead to it anytime. What I've discovered, though, is if you don't understand the deep psychological underpinnings of the program, you will screw it up, you will take shortcuts, and you will be disappointed with your results. Like many things in life, it really is easy—but it is *not* simple. That is good news, because if it were easy, your competition would have already figured it all out.

YOUR PROSPECTS ARE IRRATIONAL

The "Hidden" Side of Human Behavior

Before I show you the details of how the PSWF program works, we need to have a quick discussion about human nature. Which of the following statements do you believe to be true?

- Humans are, for the most part, rational creatures, unless strong emotions get in the way.
- Humans are emotional creatures who create their own logic to support their emotive will.

If you believe that human beings—and your prospects—are rational creatures, then I have a few follow-up questions. What about your son or daughter—are they always rational? Surely, your spouse isn't always rational? See my point? When you look at humanity as a whole, it's easy to say that humans are rational beings, but when you look at individuals up close, you see something completely different.

Over the last decade, as I read countless books researching human behavior, I learned how an energy drink sold at half price will actually be less effective—both mentally *and* physically. Medications with a higher price tag become more effective, and brand-name drugs are more effective than generics (that are chemically identical). These are collectively known as cognitive biases, and they function like blind spots for our human brains. Even when we know of their existence, we can't help but be affected by them. None of these things are rational, but they do prove that we still walk around each day mostly unaware of how our emotional world is shaping our physical one.[1]

The understanding that human beings are driven by emotion over logic is important because if you believe that your prospects'

---

1 If you want to learn more about the study of our irrationality (behavioral economics), visit *http://danariely.com/*.

behavior is driven by rational thinking, you'll be skeptical of how this program works and will be tempted to alter it.

ETHICALLY INFLUENCING YOUR PROSPECTS

The Magic of Persuasion

The PSWF program helps you guide your prospect along a desired path that results in a sale, which is done by influencing their decision-making. This isn't about manipulating people to do something that is not in their best interest. It is about using natural human behaviors to encourage those who are interested in your community to take the next step—to not get stuck in doubt or uncertainty. In his classic book, *Influence: The Psychology of Persuasion*, Dr. Robert Cialdini outlines six principles of ethical influence. Ethical influence means you are influencing while being honest and maintaining integrity.[2]

The six principles are:

1. Reciprocation
2. Scarcity
3. Authority
4. Consistency
5. Likability
6. Consensus

A Quick Example

The clearest example of ethical influence comes from the principle of reciprocity. Cialdini describes how receiving a mint with your dinner bill will result in a *3.3 percent increase* in the size of the tip you give—and that receiving two mints will increase it an average

---

2   If you want to learn more about Dr. Cialdini and his studies on ethical influence, visit *http://www.influenceatwork.com/*.

of *14.1 percent*! By giving you a free mint or two, the server is invoking the rule of reciprocity, which says that you should give back to him or her in some way. The amazing part is that even though this is a well-known statistic in the restaurant industry, 50 percent of restaurants don't give their patrons a mint with the dinner bill.

The Three Main Principles Used in PSWF

First, I want to review the three principles of ethical influence that are used repeatedly in this program. They are: **authority, scarcity,** and **consensus.** Used properly, they create a true sense of urgency that is not often felt by your prospects. Often, urgency is missing because your prospects can't tell how much demand for a new community there really is, and they believe they have all the time in the world to make a decision. But urgency is what will maximize the sales potential and profit margins for your communities.

Let's take a deeper look at the role these three principles play in influencing our prospects.

Authority

I'm starting with the easiest principle for you to apply first. The principle of authority says that people are influenced by those who display professionalism and have industry knowledge. The good news for you is that, as a home builder or developer, this is transferred to you by default (until you prove yourself not to be an authority).

We assume if someone is a doctor, they must be a good doctor (again unless proven otherwise). Similarly, because you are a home-building professional, your input matters to your prospect—even if they don't show it. They are looking to you for guidance on making a very big decision that they really don't know that much about.

Now, it is certainly true that the better your title sounds, the more innate authority your prospects will attribute to you. That is why it is imperative that you tap into those in your company at the highest level possible at key times during this process. While owners and vice presidents will have greater influence over the prospects, never underestimate the authority that you bring to the table.

After over eleven years of watching new sales reps join a builder, I have noticed that a key indicator of their success is how quickly they assume authority over the title and training they were given. Confidence can be faked, but that often comes across as being cocky. A rep with a true authoritative mindset understands that they are uniquely qualified to assist the prospect with the largest purchase of their life, and they act accordingly.

Scarcity

Value can be increased by scarcity. Oil, diamonds, and home values all fluctuate because of supply and demand. When demand outpaces supply, that scarcity creates additional value. In fact, it is the principle of scarcity that allows the number-one rule in location to be true: location, location, location. When you are able to secure an unbelievable land position in a prime location, success usually follows.

The real reason that home builders love prime locations is because the scarcity is so high it allows you to break the typical trade-off of pace and margin. When you have the hot location, you can increase your price and maintain a steady sales pace instead of seeing the sales pace slow as price increases. These communities often have pent-up demand and successful launches even without a launch process like PSWF (although they could be maximized with one). However, every location can't be an "A," so you'll need to be able to manufacture scarcity to create increased demand.

Scarcity doesn't only apply to physical products either. The same principle can apply to information. In the pages ahead, you'll see how we use the scarcity of information about a new community or phase to our advantage.

The key is to emphasize *genuine scarcity*—the fact that there is no other piece of land just like this one. Scarcity has made people get in fights over Tickle Me™ Elmo and stand in line for hours for

Apple products—and it can work even better for real estate because *everything is truly one of a kind.*

Here is a quick list of the attributes of a home site that makes each lot unique:

- Location within the community
- Size (larger is not always better)
- Corner home site
- Cul-de-sac home site
- Exposure to the sun
- Elevation
- The view
- Vegetation and trees
- Open space
- Bordering amenities
- Distance to other home sites

If we can clearly communicate what makes each home site one of a kind, then it allows your prospects to understand the reason for urgency. While you may be releasing forty or more home sites for sale, it is not a reason to take your time; there is only one "perfect" home site for each prospect.

Consensus

The principle of consensus says that people are influenced by others like them or others who they want to be like. Consensus is also commonly referred to as "herd mentality." This is why in a market for any type of product, your goal is always to be number one— because it creates additional influence over both the rest of the market and consumers.

Being number one communicates and validates to others that your product is the superior choice simply because others have already chosen you. Third-party testimonials are a favorite of marketers because that authenticity validates the message your company is trying to communicate.

Anyone can purchase an ad and make a promise to consumers. This is where the saying "buyer beware" comes from. It is easy for marketers to lie to us. However, when consensus is built around the promise a company makes, it becomes grounded and more "real" in the minds of your customers.

In this program, consensus is used to validate our assertions of genuine scarcity and is the most important ingredient. However, it is often the most misunderstood part of the program and is executed poorly. Follow each step ahead, though, and you'll master it over time. You'll even find other ways to integrate it into your general sales process with success.

The Power of Layering

When you layer all three principles outlined above—authority, scarcity, and consensus—the end result is much more powerful than any one principle by itself. The amount of demand created for your community increases exponentially. Even though these principles are better known today than ever before, their effectiveness has not changed. That's because humanity is not rational and can't help but react to these forces of influence. It is in our DNA.

PROGRAM OVERVIEW

Now that we've gone over some of the psychological background that the PSWF program is built around, let's get into the meat of the program. We'll go over the common problems and pitfalls that builders and developers face, and then I'll show you how PSWF can solve these problems and lead to great success with your community.

Common Problems and Pitfalls

This program wouldn't exist if there weren't problems that needed to be fixed, so let's look at those first. The common problems that home builders or developers need to solve tend to fall into one of three main categories:

1. **Lack of organization:** There is often little or no structure around new communities or phases, and no advanced warning when either one is to be released for sale. No one seems to have all the necessary information until moments before (or after) it is needed. You are handed the information on what to sell roughly forty-eight hours before you are asked to begin selling it.

2. **Lack of interest:** Developers are either unable or unsure of how to build a large enough interest list for the project.

3. **Lack of process:** Developers have so many people on their interest list that they don't know how to effectively communicate to buyers or nurture the list to make sure buyers are ready and willing to purchase when the grand opening occurs. Sometimes this also causes an overconfidence in the impending success of the project and a lack of urgency internally.

These struggles can vary from one individual community to another, but for those of you who have been in our industry for any length of time, you have probably experienced all of these problems at some point. Often, a lack of organization is the true root cause of the other problems. Sales and marketing departments may feel like there is little that can be properly communicated if everything is still up in the air. This is compounded by frequent delays, sometimes for years, which often occur as part of the land development process. These delays can lead to gun-shy executives who have been burned at the stake by angry prospects who feel like they have been misled or strung along.

I get it, and while working as a builder myself, I have experienced it all. The good news is that PSWF has a unique ability to adapt to the exact, unique challenge you are facing right now. We'll dive in deeper throughout the book, but I want to give you a bit more context around each of these challenges.

Lack of Organization

Turning a piece of farmland into a community is no easy task, and there are a lot of players involved. You have internal or external teams of developers who are working with the contractors doing the actual dirty work. You also have people interacting with local, regional, or national government agencies trying to get necessary approvals and sign-offs. If new plans or designs need to be developed for the community, then you also have architects, costing, purchasing, and a whole host of other groups that can slow things down or cause confusion in your ideal timeline.

With so many moving parts, teams of people, and unknown setbacks, it is good to remember that your ideal timeline will not happen. So now what?

It isn't going to run smoothly. There will be delays—or in rare cases, massive acceleration ("You now have two weeks, not six months, to get things ready!")—and you will usually have no choice but to roll with the punches. One community I worked on ended up being delayed by nearly three years from the time I already had over four hundred people on my interest list. But it didn't stress me out, because I realized that the secret to navigating setbacks successfully is to always focus on the next overall step in the process that I could control. At some point, you will be asked to begin the process of setting appointments for the sales team, but until then your only worry needs to be making sure your interest list is always growing or at least maintaining the number of qualified prospects you need.

Beyond focusing on the immediate steps that you can control, you also need to have a solid overall outline to work within. Usually when I ask someone for an outline of their current launch process, I find that nothing has been written down for the team to learn from after each attempt. You must have a written game plan that has room for the adjustments that will need to be made. The good news is that, as part of this book, I provide you with a solid framework to begin working within, but over time you may find the need to make adjustments to fit your unique culture as a builder or developer. As long as you make those adjustments fully understanding the trade-offs you are making, you will have success. I will cover each step of PSWF in detail, but sticking to a written plan and working on what you can control will greatly assist you in staying organized.

You also can't be afraid to give honest feedback. Without a minimal number of details and information, you can't proceed with a bullet-proof process. Setting expectations with your team on results and ownership based upon what they can provide you in advance is critical to your long-term career success.

Finally, make sure your team has clarity on who is ultimately in charge. Who is the quarterback of the project? Accountability and delegation of authority is absolutely necessary with the large number of moving pieces involved in successfully rolling out a new community or phase.

Lack of Interest

When people aren't rapidly choosing to join the interest list for your new community, it can be disappointing. The good news is that this is often the easiest of the three challenges to solve. If you have local data that supports the pricing, product, and positioning you are offering, the lack of interest may simply be because not enough people have been exposed to your message yet. Or, if you are building on the edge of town, or pushing pricing higher on your homes than what the competition is offering, you may have to work a little harder to find your ideal prospects. In either situation, you need to begin with the basics of new home marketing: reach and frequency.

You need to reach your ideal prospects with the highest frequency of advertising that you can afford. In today's digital world, that means Facebook and Instagram paid ads, search engine marketing (AdWords), and well-crafted landing pages. These three tactics will be the core of your strategy, and I'll cover them in greater detail later in the **Further Resources** section.

If you are already using a great core strategy, then perhaps the actual creative content of your ads is not compelling enough for your target audience. When launching a new community or phase, it is imperative to remember that this is when you get complete control to frame the story being told—and stories matter a lot. Stories help us to remember key information, share it easily with friends or coworkers, and even justify our decisions to ourselves when we second-guess them later.

Once a community has been launched, the story is outside of your control. Your prospects and visible results begin to be part of it whether you like it or not. If I drive by your empty community for a couple months, there is no way for you to communicate how well everything is going—it won't get through my BS filter. I've seen a lack of activity with my own eyes for weeks, and I no longer trust the story you are trying to sell me. This is why spending the time up front to craft a great story is worth your time, because until it launches, your story is the only one people can see or hear, and there is tremendous leverage to that truth.

Another important idea to keep in mind is that if your list isn't growing as quickly as you feel is necessary, you need to invest in your marketing budget up front to fix the problem. You may end up spending up to 30 percent or more of the marketing budget for the entire project before a single sale comes in, and that's okay. By creating the early momentum and sales results, your post-launch monthly expenses can be lower because you only need to maintain that momentum, and you have social proof of actual sales to back up your story.

Lack of Process

Sometimes the problem isn't lack of leads but too many leads and no processes in place to track them or communicate with them. The problem of having too many leads may seem like an artificial one, but it isn't. If you find yourself in a situation that truly is a "build it and they will come" scenario, don't let your guard down. Having a giant list of prospects early on doesn't mean your hard work is over. I've seen more people ultimately fail due to their lack of process than a lack of interest or organization put together.

One reason organization is still important, even if you are building in an "A" location, is because you'll get a combination of suspects, prospects, and leads reaching out to you—and it is up to you to figure out who is who. Here's an overview of each to help you organize your list and identify each party.

Suspects: These people are just curious. They may live nearby and want to keep tabs on local growth, but they have no interest in purchasing from you. Suspects tend to be completely non-responsive to your emails or calls and never give you any additional information to help you further qualify them.

Prospects: This group may respond to you from time to time, but they never seem very internally motivated. There is no urgency on their part, and they never commit to an appointment or to visiting the Preview Event. More on this event later.

Leads: These are the ones that matter. They not only respond to you but they have a high degree of motivation to take action when you offer the opportunity.

When you have a good-sized list, you have to find ways to classify each suspect, prospect, or lead. Remember, it is not our job to motivate the unmotivated. That is why we want so many people on our list. If they aren't ready to take each step, we can't stress about it but instead must focus on those people who keep raising their hand, saying, "I'm ready!"

Two giant pieces to solving the lack-of-process puzzle are having a customer relationship management (CRM) tool and a dedicated and fully accountable individual or small team to stay connected with prospects until the on-site team is ready for them. The CRM allows you to track all of the conversations (or lack thereof) with each individual who reaches out, and prompts you to take action when the time is right. For most builders or developers, the online sales consultant or inside sales rep is the right point person for the job. This individual is already equipped to communicate with hundreds of people each week through email, phone, or text message.

Giving leads over to the on-site sales team too early, too often, causes disappointment for both your prospects and the sales team. On-site sales can't help but focus on closing sales, but because the project isn't truly ready for sales yet, this creates extra friction and frustration.

We know that problems are going to come up, but hopefully now that you have the tools to identify these problems, you can also avoid them. The PSWF program will help you navigate through these common problems, and with our solutions you'll come out ahead.

KEYS TO SUCCESS

Despite lack of organization, interest, or process, PSWF allows you to have a successful community or phase launch by giving you tools to overcome each challenge. These have been refined over nearly a decade of actual use in our industry and through our involvement in launching nearly hundreds of projects across North America. This is why I promise you up to a 30 percent increase in sales results over any other process.

This program is a collection of smaller individual best practices put together into a singular comprehensive process that can easily be followed step-by-step. It is not, however, the Ten Commandments of how to launch a new community. Let me unpack that idea for you a little bit more, because it can clear up a lot of confusion.

There are no "must" or "must not" statements in this book. All communities and companies are unique, and while I am sharing the overall best practice for each step of the process, I am not saying it can't work any other way. What I hope to do is explain to you the potential risks and rewards you need to think through if you do veer off my prescribed course. You should never feel trapped or think failure is guaranteed by not hitting a milestone or task due date. PSWF is a process, but it is an organic process. It can be no other way because of the complexity of the project, amount of moving parts, and high number of stakeholders.

Model Homes Aren't That Different

Think back to the first time you were involved with the building out of a new model home. It was overwhelming and it seemed infinitely complicated—and that was if there was a documented process for you to follow and work from. If there wasn't, then you really felt like you were being set up to fail. Making sure construction is progressing on time, working with a decorator, determining the target market, selecting the options to include, and setting up a sales center—it's a lot.

Yet, after your first one or two builds, you begin to understand the rhythm of building a model home. You might even begin to adapt the existing process to make it better or create a process where it hadn't existed before. You do this because it seems like there is no other option. After all, you'll be involved with countless more model homes during your career, so you might as well have an outline of best practices.

New communities or new phases of home sites in existing communities deserve the same approach. Yet, because the amount of complexity appears to be an order of magnitude more than a model home, and because there are more outside forces you often have no control over, too many of us give up and leave each community launch to chance. In the chapters to follow, I hope to convince you that developing a process around new communities that works for you is even more important than the process for building out model homes.

The Overlap of Marketing and Sales

My business partner Mike Lyon and I often cite Mark Roberge's point that "A dysfunctional relationship between sales and marketing is the kiss of death in a buyer-driven world." Simply put, these teams need to work together. It is hard enough to get your prospect's attention and interest when things are running smoothly. When you are also battling against your internal counterparts, it can become nearly impossible. New community launches also hinge on consistent and clear communication between your company's marketing and sales departments. This is a situation that has been made much easier to solve by the rise to prominence of online sales counselors (OSC) or inside sales specialists (ISS) at the majority of homebuilding and development companies today. Throughout this book we will refer to OSC and ISS roles interchangeably. This position allows for a single individual or small team to be the single point of contact for hundreds or even thousands of interested prospects, until the project is ready for actual contracts to be written.

This also allows your on-site commissioned sales people to focus on selling what can actually be sold today. This creates less of a gap in their paycheck, and less frustration caused by inevitable delays and changes that happen during development. It also means less strain on your sales staff overall by asking them to pull double-duty on both an existing and "coming soon" community.

The OSC can be supported and trained to nurture, segment, and qualify prospects on your interest list for months, or even years, before you go to launch. Because of the strong relationships that they build over time, OSCs can then quickly activate prospects that are ready for on-site appointments.

There will be a constant tug-of-war between the sales department wanting access to these prospects as early as possible and marketing wanting to hold on to them until just the right moment. This is especially true the earlier that you involve an on-site sales person, because they want to hurry up and get selling (and can you blame them?). This can put a lot of stress on the OSC, and it requires good leadership from management to keep everyone on the same page.

The handoff from marketing to sales begins at the OSC Launch/ House in the Sky appointments (which I will detail later), where all prospects and leads are invited to meet with the on-site agents to determine their ideal home design and options. The handoff to sales is then nearly completed at the Preview Event, where everyone is invited to see the final details that have not been made available yet. You'll then know who your most motivated prospects are. After the Grand Release, you can determine if all VIP leads will be copied over into the on-site sales bucket in the CRM or will continue to be managed by the OSC until they are ready.

Now, let's get into the meat of the program. We have chosen a metaphor that will be easy for you to relate to—the phases of construction for a new home.

- **Permitting Phase** (building your list)
- **Construction Phase** (honing your list)
- **Final Walk-Through** (Preview Event)
- **Closing Table** (follow-up)

TIMELINE OVERVIEW

Before we go in depth into each phase of the program, let's take a look at an overview of the PSWF program from start to finish, and then we'll go into each step in more detail. This timeline all hinges on the Preview Event, which will be discussed later on, but for now, know that this event is what we are building up to and that it holds great importance to the entire program.

THE PERMITTING PHASE

As Early as Possible (*you can't do it too soon!*)
- Install marketing sign and put community on website (no pricing!)

Ninety Days Prior to Preview Event
- Online marketing: Facebook and Instagram ads, search engines, display ads, and syndication sites

Sixty Days Prior to Preview Event
- Direct mail to area zips: "Coming Soon" postcard #1 (optional)

Fifty Days Prior to Preview Event
- Direct mail to area zips: "Coming Soon" postcard #2 (optional)

Forty-Five Days Prior to Preview Event
- Press release sent to local media
- Blog update
- Small ad in LOCAL newspaper (optional)

THE CONSTRUCTION PHASE

Thirty Days Prior to Preview Event
- Pricing in internal system for houses only (not home site premiums)
- Begin scheduling appointments to narrow house selection
- Base house prices added to website and all online syndication sites

Twenty Days Prior to Preview Event
- Invitations to database: "You're Invited to a VIP Event" fold-over

Fifteen Days Prior to Preview Event
- Phone calls to database: "You're Invited to a VIP Event"
- Emails to database: "You're Invited to a VIP Event"

Two Days Prior to Preview Event
- Reminder emails/phone calls to RSVP list
- Video email to those who haven't responded
- Markup site map and grading map with premiums and features for each home site

THE FINAL WALK-THROUGH PHASE

PREVIEW EVENT
- Reveal grading/plat maps and timelines for development/ construction to begin. Goal is to set up appointments with new prospects, and schedule appointments to finalize home site selection with those who have already narrowed down house type.

One Day after the Preview Event
- Blog posts showing activity
- Grand opening announced publicly on website
- Hold appointments scheduled at the Preview Event with prospects. New prospects from this point forward should be given all information available and added in. Do not make them wait until after the Grand Release.

Two Days after the Preview Event
- Direct mail to database and zips: "Plat Map" (optional)
- Email to databases: "Plat Map"

THE CLOSING TABLE PHASE

GRAND RELEASE EVENT
- Completed contracts with hand money accepted on first come, first served basis

Two Days after the Grand Release
- Press release sent to local media
- Blog post
- Update all online creative on Facebook, Instagram, display, and syndication to celebrate your early success.

One to Two Weeks after the Grand Release

- Press release sent to local media
- Blog update
- Direct mail to database and zips: "We Sold X Number of Homes" postcard (optional)
- Email to databases: "We Sold X Number of Homes"

A preview party for a new community in Sewickley, PA. Over 110 attended this event for high-end luxury townhomes. It was held at a local restaurant because construction hadn't yet started on the model building.

A preview party for a master planned community in Myrtle Beach, SC. It was held at a local event space because model homes were not yet ready.

IN-DEPTH BY PHASE

THE PERMITTING PHASE

Ninety Days Prior to Preview Event (or as early as possible, if not worried about cannibalizing current offerings)
- Install marketing sign and put community on website (no pricing!)
- Online marketing: Facebook and Instagram ads, search engines, syndication sites, and display ads

Sixty Days Prior to Preview Event
- Direct mail to area zips: "Coming Soon" postcard #1 (optional)

Fifty Days Prior to Preview Event
- Direct mail to area zips: "Coming Soon" postcard #2 (optional)

Forty-Five Days Prior to Preview Event
- Press release sent to local media
- Blog update
- Small ad in LOCAL newspaper (optional)

Building Your List
This is the permitting phase of the program. The key in this phase is to combine a variety of advertising methods that overlap your

target audience to deliver a high frequency of impressions to prospects. The rule of thumb is that it takes up to seven touches before a prospect is even aware of you.

In marketing, you are always evaluating if you should be attempting to reach more people or if you should be reaching the same people with higher repetition. Your budget won't allow you to reach everyone at a high enough frequency to have an effect, so you have to choose the right balance between frequency and size. Too often, non-marketers in a building company will prioritize reach over frequency. They will say it is all a numbers game and all they need are more bodies through the door.

This is almost never the case. *You don't need more people; you need more of the right people.* In fact, overfilling the top of your sales and marketing funnel is dangerous. You will struggle with communicating to them effectively or servicing them as well as you would like. You'll also have to increase your overhead to deal with the inefficiency of the approach. You want to prioritize reaching your best prospects in as many ways as possible in order to gain awareness with them and them only. Over time, this will not only create larger awareness but will also lead to increased brand loyalty.

Marketing Sign

This is the large sign placed at the entrance of your community. It should include the name of the builder and community, a phone number, your website, and "coming soon" verbiage. It should NOT include pricing, release dates, or detailed product information.

Putting the sign up first allows those who are already in your geographic area to build awareness. They may or may not be demographically or psychographically the right match, but it will generate buzz in the local area that you will use to your advantage.

Website

The community page should include a contact phone number and email address, an invitation to join a VIP list for priority information, and the unique selling points of the community/surrounding area (school districts, general home site sizes, etc.). It should NOT contain any pricing, specific product information, or any community layout/site map information so that the scarcity of information ensures that people attend the preview party. *Keep it simple*, and have an easy way for prospects to take action and sign up for the VIP list on the page itself, instead of having to go to a separate contact form.

If your website isn't flexible enough to allow a page like this to be created, consider creating a stand-alone landing page specific for your community. Landing pages are customized for specific purposes and don't have to have the same structure as the rest of your site. They should still be branded well, but they can be a great way to get the result you need without doing major work on the back end of your site. The **Further Resources** section at the end of this book covers landing pages in more depth.

Online Marketing

Your own website should be your highest converting source of leads; however, the right online marketing program can create more qualified traffic to your website. There are four main groups you'll be concerned with in this program:

- Search engines: Google, Yahoo, Bing, etc.
- Syndication sites: Trulia, Zillow, NewHomeSource, etc.
- Display ads: targeted banner ads and remarketing
- Social media: Facebook and Instagram

You should approach each of these as a way to tease interest in the new property. Since you are withholding pricing, it can be difficult to get results from syndication just yet. However, doing the legwork to get it ready to go without pricing will allow you to move faster when the time is right. For more information on social media, check out the **Social Media** section on page 51.

Direct Mail

Ever since email and digital marketing became popular, direct mail has fallen out of favor with most people who consider themselves "marketing experts." We all receive less of it today than we did just a few years ago. Even those "I just sold your neighbor's house" post-cards from general brokerage agents are disappearing. This void creates an opportunity for your direct mail piece to get more attention simply because mailboxes are less cluttered. Let me be clear, online marketing is priority number one. If your budget ever makes you choose between online and direct mail, choose online. However, this is still a great optional medium to add in to your mix.

Highly targeted mail pieces are like the Marines in your army of awareness. They may not be as sexy as the Air Force, but you can't win a war from the air. You need boots on the ground, and direct mail is the perfect first wave of attack. More important than the overall design that is on your postcard, is the list to which the postcard is being sent. That's why at my company, Do You Convert, we use a direct mail program that allows you to go way beyond picking a zip code or a community to send your message to. This specific targeting can be done by most direct mail vendors today.

By analyzing data from your past customers, you can create a *house-by-house list* of those you should be targeting instead of going by entire streets, communities, or zip codes. The data will let you see what kind of people are most likely to purchase a home from you. They are predisposed to want what you are offering and to connect with your brand. Even if they don't purchase a home from you, these are the people who will amplify your message by sharing it with their friends, coworkers, and family because they still connect with you.

This truly is a game changer and is rooted in deep research and analysis. When I work with builders or even sales reps who are skeptical about direct mail's effectiveness, the results we see from TruTarget change their mind.

If you aren't able to take advantage of TruTarget mailings, then the rest of this section will give you the criteria to consider when building your list:

- Geography (zip code, postal route, county, community)
- Demographics
- Household income
- Household age
- Number of adults
- Number of children
- Current dwelling
- Owner/renter
- Length of residence
- Year built
- Home value
- Interests and lifestyles
- Credit card types
- Hobbies/interests

Your goal is to narrow your list to only include your target market. Your budget will affect how many mailings you are able to send out, but you never want the number of households selected to be less than one thousand. Start with geography and then add on income, age, and other variables to lower your numbers until you're satisfied you have the absolute best one thousand or more households to target.

Old-school marketers will tell you to use communities or neighborhoods as your geographic limit, but I've found them not to be as effective as widening your geography to at least the zip code level and using the criteria listed above to bring the numbers down. After all, if my ideal prospect happens to live two blocks from a specific neighborhood, why wouldn't I want to include them?

Finally, at a minimum, you want to hit that same list at least two times (three or four is even better if your budget allows—even if you need to shrink the list size a bit). You only need to make minimal changes to the artwork for each mailing. The main thing is to build impressions and word of mouth among your target market so your other awareness efforts are more successful.

Local Advertising

This is an easy and low-cost way to create additional awareness within your targeted geographic footprint. Do not waste your money with the large newspapers (although your press release may still get you some FREE exposure in them!), but instead focus on lower-cost local newspapers where the readership will be more interested in your offering.

Press Releases

Your press release should include the name of your community, its location, and any other information you have on floor plan size and unit numbers. Also make sure to include contact information for anyone interested in joining the VIP list for priority information. This will help create buzz early on. When it's time to send out your press releases, like the local advertising mentioned above, target local newspapers. Don't forget to put the press release on your blog and social media outlets as well!

Blog Update

A regularly updated blog will help generate interest and will provide a great place to update potential buyers. During the PSWF program, your blog posts should match the rest of your marketing calendar. Any information sent out in emails and press releases can also go up on your blog. Think of this as a "countdown" approach: as the launch gets closer, add additional posts about different parts of the process. Examples of blog posts include: "Get to Know Your New Neighborhood," "VIP Event Information," and "Community Sneak Peeks."

No Lead Left Behind

As you begin to generate awareness of the project, the leads will begin to flow in. Without a doubt, the best practice is to have those leads go to an OSC or ISS in your organization. Their job is to make sure all leads are entered into your CRM system, are properly organized, and are consistently communicated to through a drip marketing campaign.

Getting these leads to your sales team in the field too early can be detrimental because it will distract them from selling homes in communities that are open for sale today, and the organizational skills to handle the large volume of inquiries is not usually a strong suit of your best sales people. If you don't have an OSC, then simply designate a single person to be in charge of all incoming prospects and ask them for weekly updates on the size of your VIP list, so you can adjust your awareness strategy as needed.

THE CONSTRUCTION PHASE

Thirty Days Prior to Preview Event
- Pricing in internal system for houses only (not home site premiums)
- Begin scheduling appointments to narrow house selection
- Base house prices added to website and all online syndication sites

Twenty Days Prior to Preview Event
- Invitations to database: "You're Invited to a VIP Event" fold-over

Fifteen Days Prior to Preview Event
- Phone calls to database: "You're Invited to a VIP Event"
- Postcard invitation to all databases: "You're Invited to a Sneak Preview!"
- Emails to database: "You're Invited to a VIP Event"

Two Days Prior to Preview Event
- Reminder email/phone calls to RSVP list
- Video email to those who haven't responded
- Markup site map and grading map with premiums and features for each home site

Honing Your List

In the next phase of the program, you are layering the large brush strokes of awareness from the previous phase with additional touch points for those who have already expressed interest. In addition, as soon as base pricing for the homes is ready, the sales team can begin to have *preliminary* meetings with prospects to narrow down the house that best fits the prospect's needs. Once the pricing updates are live, your OSC can begin to reach out to everyone on the VIP list to schedule as many pricing appointments for the house as possible.

It is crucial that *the majority of those attending the Preview Event have already narrowed down their house type.* This prevents any slowdown in emotional excitement after they see the home sites (i.e., you don't want to have to say, "Okay, now let's determine the house type that's right for you," after they select their home site at the event). It also allows you to be more strategic about how you demonstrate the home sites to them. For more information on narrowing down their house type, see the **House in the Sky** section.

Add Pricing to Internal Systems

Thirty days prior to the Preview Event, you'll want your sales team to add pricing into your internal system. Your sales team will want to begin to schedule preliminary pricing appointments with prospects to select the house type and structural options of their home. It should be made clear to the prospect that pricing is not final and may adjust minimally at the Preview Event.

Pricing should also not include any home site premiums or adjustments because this information will not be shared until the preview party. The sales team needs to communicate that doing this prep work ahead of time will allow customers to act quickly to secure their ideal home site once it is available. Your sales team should also be keeping detailed notes about customers' "hot buttons" and what their ideal home sites look like.

It is not critical that the home be 100 percent priced out, as decorator details can be completed later. You do, however, want to be sure that the sales team understands the structural options desired so that the home sites you "walk" on paper at the Preview Event are an ideal fit.

Add Base Prices to Your Website

Adding the base prices to your website now allows you to market effectively on real estate syndication websites like Trulia, Zillow, NewHomeSource, etc. It also allows you to send an email update to those on the VIP list and encourage them to set an appointment to do initial pricing. Once you send that message out, be sure your staff is ready to react quickly to customers.

Invitations

I'm always shocked at how people work the invitation process of any event. Usually, a single invitation is sent out and it's assumed that those invited treasure the invitation like an award. Surely they put it in a place of prominence in their home just so they can see it as they walk by each day, right?

Nope.

This isn't because they aren't interested (remember, they signed up for more information!) but more so because people are busy and need reminders. Use multiple methods (snail mail, email, phone, and text) to send the invite for the Preview Event, but only send one additional reminder to those who have already RSVP'd.

Professional fold-over invitations (think wedding invitations) should be sent to those on the VIP list, and a less expensive postcard version should be sent to all your existing databases. Let them know that exclusive information will be shared at the Preview Event and will include when development work will be complete, home site release dates, and site map layouts.

Markup Site Map and Grading Map

After you've had preliminary pricing appointments, you can put to work the information you've already learned. Having an internal prep meeting where you mark up your site map with information will be valuable prep for the House in the Sky meeting and Preview Event, both discussed later in this book. You already know what homes your best prospects are interested in, so you can add notes to your maps that will guide them to the home sites you think are best for them.

You can also create additional urgency by adding notes such as "best home site for floor plan X," "perfect for a walkout basement," etc.

Use the hot buttons that your prospects have already shared with you, and make sure each home site comes across as being unique in some way. These should be written on large poster-size copies that can be displayed with an easel at the Preview Event. You'll want to have multiple copies of both the grading and layout maps, depending on the crowd you are expecting.

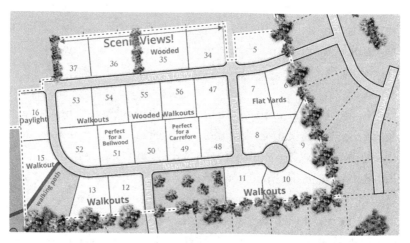

Add details on the map based on feedback from your house in the sky discussion on key motivators for different prospects.

The grading map is important because it gives you more information that will allow you to "walk" the home site on paper with the prospect. This data can help you paint the picture of what it will feel like to live on that home site. This is especially important in markets with heavier terrain and grade changes. It will also convey your extensive knowledge, as even well-informed prospects will have a tough time reading a grading map properly.

Depending on the number of those who have had pricing appointments, this prep meeting may take you thirty minutes or several hours. Don't skimp. You can direct people to home sites that are best for them. It also helps you not to stack three prospects on the same home site. When you are done, you should have a list with the names of each prospect as well as the following information:

- Homes priced out/price ranges
- Best home for them (per sales rep)
- Hot buttons
- Prequalified (yes/no)
- House to sell (yes/no)
- Main objections
- Time frame

Make enough copies of this information for each person who will be working your event. This will keep everyone on the same page and give a consistent message to each prospect.

TRANSITIONING FROM OSC TO ON-SITE SALES TEAM

A Single Point of Contact

Up until this point, prospects and VIPs have likely only interacted with a single point of contact or small team within your company. This is done for three important reasons:

- It allows members of your on-site sales team to remain focused on other opportunities to sell homes that are available today instead of using their energy to nurture people along a longer process. Traditional sales people will grow frustrated and anxious if they are asked to invest their time on people for months without ever asking them to buy (or telling them they need to wait for the launch). It can also lead to a rather large dip in their paycheck if they are predominantly paid on commission.
- Having only one point of contact or small team gives you greater control over the release of information. The release of updated information is a large part of what makes the PSWF program successful. You need to be careful with how many people have access to information and when they get it. If key

elements of the project leak out to the public too early, it can kill your urgency-building efforts.

- All prospects are given a consistent message, which can help to eliminate guesswork about what has or has not been communicated to everyone.

At Do You Convert, our preferred point of contact is an online sale counselor (OSC) or ISS. My partner Mike Lyon and I believe this position is so important in today's world that he wrote an entire book about it: *Browsers to Buyers: Proven Strategies for Selling New Homes Online.*

The Handoff

As the project gains momentum, the handoff from the OSC to the on-site sales team can become an elephant in the room, which may begin to grow larger and larger. Because the single point of contact is someone who is not actually going to lead the sales effort, it can cause consternation with those who do. They want access to the VIP list early and often. They can't help it! They are good sales people and know that until they connect with the list, they have no opportunity to advance the sale.

The reality is that giving traditional sales people access to this list too early can be disastrous because the prospects aren't ready to be sold and will not behave in the same manner that they would if they walked into a furnished model home with standing inventory. To make matters worse, our research and time with clients at Do You Convert has led to the understanding that most on-site sales people are not clear and effective communicators over the phone or email. Their reliance on body language and instant feedback as part of a sales presentation doesn't apply without the face-to-face connection and can throw them out of their peak performance zone.

However, there is a clear point in the PSWF process where we will begin to hand off to the on-site sales team prospects that are ready. It is called the OSC Launch, and it occurs when you are ready to begin communicating detailed product information and allow prospects to schedule private one-on-one meetings with the sales team to get more detailed information for their specific preferences.

This handoff signals a change in pacing for the process as well. Up until this point, we have moved consistently and methodically through different list-building phases. But once the OSC Launch occurs and the prospects are able to begin engaging more directly with the OSC and the on-site sales team, the pace will quicken significantly. Don't launch until you're ready for this and have your information as close to finalized as possible.

The OSC Launch

The OSC Launch is a series of communications from the OSC or ISS to everyone on the VIP list. They are sharing the first clear specifics on the product for the new community. Up until this point, everything has been general—ranges of square footage, standard features that will apply to all home types, etc. The goal is to allow those who are ready to begin taking the next step and begin making choices related to the home itself.

Remember, in PSWF, we separate the choices to be made into two groups: choices around the home itself, and choices around the home site/location of the home within the community.

Once the home types and base prices have been loaded onto your website, the OSC will begin by sending an email to everyone on the list, making sure they are the first to know that the information is available to view. It will also include the ability for those interested to schedule private appointments with the on-site sales team to begin to narrow down their options and get more detailed specifics on options and upgrades available. See the sample email below.

Hello, [Registrant First Name],

Today's the day—it's here! *As a member of our VIP list for [Community Name], I'm thrilled to let you know that the home design details and introductory pricing for the community is now available to view on our website. Just click here: [Insert Link to Community Page].*

I'm also excited to let you know that, effective immediately, I can also schedule you a private appointment with [Sales Rep Name], the sales manager for [Community Name]. He/She will be able to help you determine the home design that will perfectly meet your unique needs. He/She will also be able to give you option pricing and additional details not available on the website.

Due to the overwhelming demand we've received regarding [Community Name], these appointments will be scheduled on a first come, first served basis. *Feel free to give me a call at [Insert Phone], or simply reply to this email and I'll assist you as quickly as possible. Scheduling this appointment truly allows you to remain in the driver's seat and take full advantage of your VIP status.*

(Assuming you will be holding a VIP Event, add in this next part as well.)

Finally, save the date of [Insert Date] on your calendar. Our VIP Preview Event will be held at [Location] to allow us to give you any remaining details not yet finalized and made available. You'll also have the opportunity to meet the owners and managers at [Insert Location] in a fun and relaxed atmosphere.

As always, if you have any questions at all, don't hesitate to connect with me. I'm here to help!

[Signature]

Why send an email first? It makes sure all those on the VIP list have an equal opportunity to respond. It also allows you to gauge the overall health of your database. Often, this email alone can cause an overwhelming response if the list has been nurtured properly. If it doesn't, then the OSC can continue with additional communication options to generate more interest. Phone calls and video emails to those on your list that don't respond to the launch email are ideal. Use clues found in your CRM to help you prioritize who should get that extra phone call or email from you. Look at web-tracking details (are they going back on your website regularly?) as well as email marketing reports (are they opening or clicking on your emails?) to determine who is most likely to convert.

It is important that the OSC has the ability to set up pricing appointments on a pre-determined calendar. This eliminates any back-and-forth needed to schedule pricing appointments and improves conversion rates. You also will want to determine in advance how long you want each appointment to be scheduled for. We'll review more detailed information on how these meetings should be run in the following section as well.

After a few days to a week have gone by, if you still feel like you need more people to take the next step, you can repeat this process with all of the non-VIP leads in your CRM—even if they originally requested information on another community. This is a key element to companies that run the PSWF program well: they are always adding new, fresh leads into the database, even leading up to the day of the Grand Release. They are never satisfied with "enough" interest. So, keep promoting the VIP process on social media, email newsletters, websites, etc., and then catch those leads up with everyone else as quickly as possible.

Typically, this launch takes place about thirty days prior to your Preview Party date. This gives the on-site team enough time to meet one-on-one with every prospect that has expressed interest. You may need more or less time, depending on the number of home sites being released or prospects that express interest. Internally, your sales team and OSC should refer to these appointments as "House in the Sky" meetings. We'll unpack exactly why that is in the following section.

The House in the Sky Appointment

When the OSC Launch occurs, the primary goal is to schedule as many House in the Sky appointments as possible. To prospects, these are "pricing appointments" where they can find out all the specifics of their favorite floor plan. As an overview, the goal of these meetings are:

- To allow the prospect to become more invested in the community by learning as many details about the floor plans, options, and upgrades as they can. This allows them to have a better understanding of the range that their final price will likely be in, as well as which floor plan will meet their needs.
- To allow the sales rep to begin building their own rapport with the prospect who, up until now, has been communicating with the OSC. They also can uncover the deeper reasons and motivations of the buyer and their financial situation, and help guide them through the product offering.
- To allow the sales rep to uncover the prospect's preferences relating to the home site. While this information will not be released until the VIP Preview Event, it won't stop the prospect from asking questions related to the site map, home sites, premiums, etc. When they ask, this is the opportunity for the sales rep to take notes on their preferences, which will be crucial to the success of the VIP Preview Event.

Making Decisions Easier

In the PSWF program, we simplify the process by separating the two main decisions that prospects will need to make. Separating the decisions also allows us to stay one step ahead by learning more about what the prospect desires without revealing more information to them.

These two decisions are:

- **What to build:** The floor plan to be built. Will it meet their needs? How can they personalize it? What does the process look like?
- **Where to build:** Where should their ideal home be located? What is the best fit for the type of home they will live in and options they have chosen? Can they afford a premium home site? Do they want a big yard or less maintenance? What direction do they want their patio to face?

These appointments are called House in the Sky meetings because the on-site sales team will review all the details about what to build without any land details (where to build) attached to it—as if it were "in the sky." The size of the home site, location, premiums, direction, etc., is not relevant at this point in the process, except to uncover their preferences, which you can use later on to keep them focused on the best home sites for them.

What to Cover and What to Skip (for now)

Due to the potentially high number of House in the Sky meetings your on-site sales person will need to hold, you want to keep the meeting focused and efficient. Most companies will find that an hour for this initial meeting is long enough to help the prospect narrow down their favorite home design and to review main structural options. While this won't give them a final price, it will usually get them close enough to determine if they are likely to be outside their comfort level or not. If needed, additional appointments can always be scheduled with the prospect; however, make sure you prioritize getting in each prospect for this first meeting before adding additional ones. Design studio options like cabinets, countertops, etc., can all be made at a later date and can be a real time suck if you attempt to cover it all now.

Tell Them What's Next

When your prospects leave the House in the Sky meeting, they should:

- Have a preferred home design and have a list of structural options to consider if they have not already finalized their decisions
- Have an understanding of how the process works from this point forward
    - Pricing appointment: understand product/pricing
    - VIP Preview Event: details on home sites/site plan/ premiums
    - Walk their preferred home site/finalize paperwork
    - Grand Release Event: turn in completed contracts and secure their selections

It is worth spending time reviewing the process to come so prospects don't become overwhelmed or nervous. As they begin to fall more in love with the ideas you are sharing with them, it is natural for them to also become more anxious because they will have a fear of losing out on getting what they want. Reassure them that this process is in place to give them the time they need to make an informed decision and not feel added stress.

As soon as the prospect leaves the meeting, the sales rep needs to compile all their notes into the CRM or a spreadsheet that lists the details of all their House in the Sky meetings with each prospect. This will allow the final bit of marketing magic to occur at the final planning meeting for the VIP Preview Event that comes next.

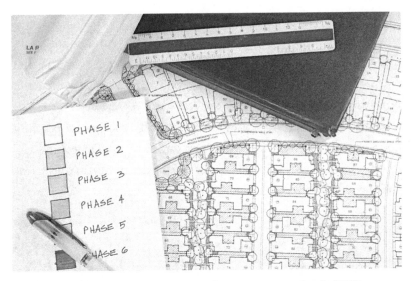

A rule of thumb is one marked-up site map for every 8–10 people who RSVP.

THE FINAL WALK-THROUGH PHASE

PREVIEW EVENT

Reveal grading/plat maps and timelines for development/construction to begin. The goal is to set up appointments with new prospects and schedule appointments to finalize home site selection with those who have already narrowed down house type.

One Day after the Preview Event
- Blog posts showing activity
- Grand opening announced publicly on website
- Hold appointments scheduled at the Preview Event with prospects. New prospects from this point forward should be given all information available and added in. Do not make them wait until after the Grand Release.

Two Days after the Preview Event
- Direct mail to database and zips: "Plat Map" (optional)
- Email to databases: "Plat Map"

Activating Your List

You have spent all of this time building your list and honing your list, and now it's finally time to let your list do your work for you. This is the most important phase of the entire process, which contains the most important event as well—the Preview Event. Don't be fooled by the name. This "preview" is actually your grand opening, and you need to prepare and perform for it as such. Do it right, and it will make the Grand Release day one of the most fun and stress-free days of your sales career.

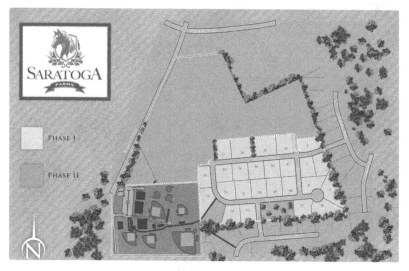

A sample of a marketing site map that hides additional details on future phases to keep the focus on the phase being released.

Preview Event

This is it. The entire PSWF program hinges on the Preview Event. Of utmost importance is simply getting the attendance for this event to be as high as possible. Even if only 25 percent of the attendees are truly interested, they won't know that the other 75 percent aren't. However, you should not fill the event with real estate professionals and employees—prospects are very good at picking out people who simply don't belong. My experience has shown that somewhere between 30–60 percent of those who attend this event will purchase within one week of the Grand Release.

The number of people attending validates all the messages of urgency and scarcity in each prospect's mind. At every Preview Event I have attended, someone says to me: "It is simply amazing that in today's economy you have gotten a turnout like this. It's unbelievable." Even as the market has improved, the impact has been the same.

Most companies make the mistake of having a private one-on-one appointment with people on their VIP list, where all of the information is shared and they attempt to make a sale right away. The problem is that once the prospect has all of the information, they are in control—and without seeing all of the other prospects, the urgency remains low. You can tell prospects that interest is high until you are blue in the face, but they won't really believe you because, after all, you're the sales person. On the other hand, they can't ignore all the other prospects at the preview party, and it will grow their fear of loss.

It is also a good idea to have the owner of the company or high-level managers at the event. Their ability to *influence prospects with their authority* (see page 4) shouldn't be underestimated—especially at this event. If necessary, have someone from your company train everyone on how to "walk" home sites on paper to give them an idea of yard sizes, views, etc., after the home is placed on-site. You'll also need enough sales people there so that no prospects are ignored.

There is another aspect of human nature that will help you at the event. We all assume everyone else is similar to us. We expect people to like the same food, watch the same television shows, use the same parenting techniques, etc. *This adds to the urgency* because the prospects will assume that there are others at the party interested in their favorite home site and their favorite home design. You don't need to tell them otherwise.

Do not attempt to hold appointments or complete contracts at the Preview Event!

Your goal is to schedule follow-up appointments to finalize the details. Doing so keeps you in control, and everyone still feels like they have the opportunity to get their first choice. As people realize they can't secure anything right away, you'll feel the tension build. Make sure to take photos of the event to post on your blog and social media outlets.

Appointments to Finalize Paperwork

These appointments will allow your prospects to walk in on the day of the Grand Release, give you a check, and put their signatures on the contract. This will allow you to get through multiple contract appointments quickly in the same day (along with additional help from others in the company). You'll also be able to use it as an opportunity to push people to home sites that you know another qualified party wants. What happens if two prospects want the same home site? Let them know that priority goes to the prospect that has a clean contract, includes full hand money, is prequalified, and is not contingent. Beyond that, it is first come, first served.

Direct Mail and Email of Plat Map

The purpose of these mailings is to share the information that was missed by those who did not attend the event, and to remind those who did attend of the urgency to move forward. You'll want to schedule this to hit just a couple days after your event. For snail mail, this will mean proper planning ahead of time.

A preview party for a new place at a community in Moon Twp, PA. Over 14 homes were sold in the first weekend.

THE CLOSING TABLE PHASE

GRAND RELEASE EVENT

- Completed contracts with hand money accepted on first come, first served basis

Two Days after the Grand Release

- Press release sent to local media
- Blog update
- Update all online creative on Facebook, Instagram, display, and syndication to celebrate your early success

One to Two Weeks after the Grand Release

- Press release sent to local media
- Blog update
- Direct mail to database and zips: "We Sold X Number of Homes" postcard (optional)
- Email to databases: "We Sold X Number of Homes"

Appreciating Your List

After all of your hard work and preparation, it is time to *sell a lot of houses!*

Grand Release Event

The hard work of your team pays off today. You'll start the day having a good idea of how many prospects will be attending to finalize their purchase, but don't be surprised when a few additional ones show up. You'll want to make sure you have extra staff on hand to make it a quick and painless process for everyone.

Spread the Good News

Make sure you spread the news far and wide about your results. You'll want to use most—if not all—of the same methods that you used for your awareness campaign at the beginning. You'll be able to use headlines such as "35 Percent of Phase II Sold in First Day! Don't Miss This Opportunity!" For your prospects that were on the fence, this urgency will help to push them over.

Even those who are part of your target market but have never interacted with you at all will be surprised to learn about your results. This can generate terrific word of mouth and lead to referrals of friends and family they know who are searching for a new home. Even if they don't have firsthand experience, they will likely mention you because they assume the sales rate proves that it's a great place to live (principle of consensus).

CONCLUSION

Wrap-Up and Encouragement

The first time you implement PSWF, you're going to feel nervous. It will feel similar to the first time you tried a particular closing technique—unnatural and awkward.

The way that the psychology of this system works means you'll have prospects begging you to sign a contract earlier in the process—or at least to put something on hold before the Preview Event. This should be your mental note to trust the process, *not to get nervous and shortcut it for a sale or two.* Follow it from beginning to the end the first time, then learn and adapt it as needed to fit your product or company.

FURTHER RESOURCES

SOCIAL MEDIA

How Facebook and Instagram Can Solve Almost Any Problem

If you're facing a marketing problem, Facebook and Instagram can help you solve it. It can help increase online traffic; it can get more people to your model home; and it can tell you how much you should be paying for your next development, what your exterior elevations should look like, and so much more. For PSWF, we will be using Facebook to make sure that those who are most likely to respond to the new community offering will know that it even exists. While many prospects may actively seek out details on your project, many more will be unaware that it is on the horizon until you let them know it is coming. Beyond awareness, we can also use Facebook to remarket to those who have already signed up to become a VIP, and we can continue to nurture them along with updates and additional video or photographic content as it is developed.

The incredible part is that, compared to other marketing channels, Facebook can do all these things for a fraction of the cost. That is why I consider Facebook's platform to be the largest advertising game changer since Google invented AdWords. Yes, there are other platforms—Twitter, Snapchat, and others—but only Facebook and Instagram have proven their ability to drive real sales results at scale, so we'll only be focusing on those here.

The clock is ticking on paid social media advertising, because as more and more companies realize the opportunity, demand will rapidly increase costs. Early adopters of AdWords used to spend 10¢ per click on keywords like "new homes," and now you could easily pay $3–$10 or more, depending on the market you serve. Facebook ads will likely follow a similar pattern. In fact, many of our clients in "hot" markets have seen their expenses for paid social media ads double over the past year.

First, I want to give you a quick overview on the different types of Facebook ads you should be most concerned about. Then we'll look at how they can be applied to the PSWF program and the ideal way to target the audience for each. **By the time this book is printed, the Facebook ad platform will likely have undergone major changes, so I encourage you to visit DoYouConvert.com and search for "Facebook" in the search box to view the latest updates and recommendations.**

Facebook Ad Types

Traffic: Traffic-driving ads have a singular goal of getting people to visit a website on their device. Traffic ads come in lots of different content packages—single photo, multiple photo (carousel), and video. The ultimate success of these campaigns comes down to your audience-targeting and the page on your website (or landing page) to which you send people. For instance, traffic ads push the Facebook user off of the platform and to your own website or app.

Engagement: This ad type prioritizes engagement with the content from within Facebook itself. Viewing your image in detail, commenting, liking, or sharing are all considered to be "engagement." If you include a link in your description, you can also get traffic to your site, but Facebook will prioritize engagement that stays on Facebook first. If you want to get hundreds of "likes" or hearts on a post at a low cost, this is the one for you. The latest studies that we've done at DoYouConvert.com also show that it may be the most efficient campaign type overall. This is because the engagement focus gets a lot of social proof (likes, hearts, comments, etc.) to travel alongside your marketing message, leading to more clicks on the link away from Facebook, even though the link itself is not as front and center as it appears within the traffic-driving ads.

Video Views: The name says it all. This format delivers your videos to those most likely to watch or engage with them. A word of caution is that Facebook considers three seconds of viewing time to equal a "view," so don't get too excited when you see the view count skyrocket. You'll need to dig a little deeper in the reporting to see how many people watched a significant portion of your content. A large percentage of videos are also watched without sound, so be sure to take advantage of Facebook's built-in caption option so people can still follow along.

Lead Generation: This one really gets the marketers excited but can also cause the most frustration with your sales team if done incorrectly. Lead generation ads allow prospects to share their contact information with you directly from Facebook and drop it into your CRM without ever visiting your website. It is not uncommon to see an average cost per lead of less than $5 from lead generation ads. The challenge is that because Facebook makes it so easy for people to share their information (it will auto-populate the form with their Facebook profile data), they often don't realize they are sharing it! Remember, we aren't just looking for lead quantity but also high lead quality.

If you aren't having any challenge growing your list without lead ads, then don't be in a rush to add this tactic to your campaign mix. However, if you need a shot in the arm with your list-building efforts, lead ads are fantastic.

The Best Ways to Target Your Prospects

There are infinite ways to slice and dice the database of Facebook and Instagram users to uncover those most likely to take action, but after spending over $1 million in ads on these platforms, we've been able to build a list of best practices that I want to share with you. The goal is to target the largest number of prospects that your budget will allow, while also making the list as specific to your ideal customer as possible. This will help to stretch your ad dollar and allow you to make the ads themselves more engaging to your audience.

Geography: This should be the first filter you apply, and it is fairly straightforward. The most critical component is not to create geographic areas that are beyond where your prospects are likely to come from. In other words, focus on smaller cities rather than larger ones (i.e., Dublin or Hilliard, Ohio, instead of Columbus, Ohio), or use the "drop pin" ability to place small circles (as small as a one-mile radius) around your ideal spots.

Additionally, you can determine if you want to target everyone in a specific location or only those who live in or have recently traveled to the locations you select. These options can be important if you believe your community will draw people from out of town or only those who are already local.

Age and Sex: The most important tip I can give you here is to select an age range five years younger and older than you want. If someone matches all the other criteria you are looking for (including being able to afford your product) but they are two years under your ideal demographic, you don't want to miss out on reaching them. So, if you typically think of your buyers being between thirty-five and fifty-five, select a range of thirty to sixty to get the best results.

When it comes to focusing on males or females, it depends on your budget. If you can afford to go after both, you should. However, if you need to scale down your audience after you complete all of these sections, then choose to target females first. They tend to interact more with social ads about real estate and are also generally regarded as the "change agents" in a relationship that will lead the hunt for a new home.

Income: This is the most straightforward selection that you'll need to make. You'll want to select income ranges that fall within what a buyer must be earning in order to qualify for your new home. The only exceptions are age-targeted communities where it may make more sense to target based on liquid assets or net worth. Thankfully, both are optional choices in this category.

Interests: Beyond the basic demographic items listed above, you can target Facebook or Instagram users based on thousands of other criteria. You will want to spend some time doing your own research, but the items listed below are some of our favorite selections.

- **Likely to move** (behaviors → residential profiles): "People who are very likely to move residences"
- **Six or more years** (behaviors → residential profiles → length of residence): "Length of time that the surname has been at this particular address"
- **Renters** (demographics → home → home ownership): "People who rent their home"
- **Zillow** (interests → additional interests): "People who have expressed an interest in or like pages related to Zillow"
- **Employer** (demographics → work → employers): "People who listed their employer as the company you choose." Most larger corporations will have enough employees to make the list. This is one section where you can't simply browse a list of options, because there are too many to choose from. If you wanted to target employees of FedEx, you'd simply type "FedEx" into the search box and select the option for "FedEx

– Employed By." (Be careful! You may also be presented with "FedEx – Interests," which would be people who have liked the FedEx page—a completely different audience.)

- **Other community-specific interests:** If your community has an amenity or feature that you think will draw people in, be sure to use that feature to inform other areas to target. Examples include: golf, swimming, childcare, etc.

You'll also want to take advantage of retargeting those who have already visited your website using "custom audience" options within the ad platform. You currently have two main options: look-alike audiences and custom audiences.

- **Look-alike audiences:** These allow you to reach new people who are similar to your current audience. It will take an existing list from your CRM, or manual input you share, to determine the top 1 percent of the population that look most like your ideal prospect.
- **Custom audiences:** Create lists of people based on one-to-one matches of your CRM database, website traffic (remarketing), or engagement on other ads you are already running (i.e., those who already acted on a lead ad or previously clicked on an ad and spent time on your site).

Match Your Creative with Your Audience

Outside of the basics, this is the most important concept to understand when diving into the world of paid social media advertising. Your ads themselves must be unique enough to match the exact targeting you have selected for each campaign. If you are targeting renters, your ad headline and imagery need to be speaking directly to renters. If you target move-up buyers who have lived in their current home for more than six years, you need to speak to that group specifically. Generic ads need not apply. There is no getting around it.

By using the context of your target audience to inform what your ad says and the way it looks, you'll get far superior results.

Don't be afraid to use representative images from other projects in your social media ads when you don't have anything else ready.

Launch and Then Adjust

The magic of paid social media advertising is how fast you can see the initial results. You'll want to give your ads forty-eight to seventy-two hours to build up momentum on the platforms, but if they aren't taking off, you can adjust quickly. Keep testing and analyzing your results until you find your personal sweet spot between cost and effectiveness. Be wary of agencies or partners who tell you that the campaign needs a longer ramp-up period in order to tell if it is working.

Don't be afraid to pause campaigns after a while, but don't be in a rush to delete any. You want to make sure you can compare data on multiple campaigns over time, so you know for certain which are most effective.

LANDING PAGES

Are you struggling to generate leads from your website for a new community? Or perhaps your current website doesn't allow you to format a well-displayed "coming soon" community because it requires information you don't yet want to give away? You can always spend more of your marketing budget to get new leads—but after a certain point, that cost per lead gets to be too high. Assuming that your Facebook and Google AdWords are set up correctly and performing well, what do you do? Create landing pages.

So, let's get technical: What is a landing page and what does it do? Simply put, a landing page is the first page someone sees on your website after clicking your ad. In the context of this book, when we say "landing page," we mean a specifically designed page with the sole purpose of converting that visit into a lead. Yes—every single page of our website should have an easy-to-find and enticing call-to-action button. But on a landing page, the only option for a visitor is to leave or become a lead.

And you know what? They work! We've seen pages that consistently convert up to 18 percent of viewers.

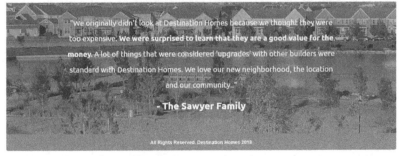

How do you get started?

You can build landing pages into your current website or you can use a third-party tool. What matters most is getting results. Either option is fine, but we're partial to using a tool. Using a tool gives you so much more control over layout and functionality without needing to have strong IT skills.

I personally love the Unbounce tool for building landing pages. It's very simple to use and integrates with almost every CRM out there (including Lasso!), so you'll be sure that no lead is left behind. Unbounce has plans starting around $100/month. You'll find that most of the landing-page builders are around this same cost.

To set up Unbounce, all you need to do is either create a sub-domain for your current website or purchase a new domain that you'll use exclusively for landing pages. Either way, the IT portion of the setup should only take a few minutes. Best of all, it won't disrupt your website.

When should you use landing pages?

Your goal rate for converting visitors to new leads should be between 1.5 and 2 percent. Break this down by community and submarket to determine which areas are struggling to generate leads. Keep in mind this could be happening for a number of reasons outside of your control—like pricing and where homes are being built.

Sometimes a dedicated landing page is the best choice no matter what. However, there are many other situations where the decision is up in the air. So how do you know whether to use your website or a landing page?

There are many situations where using a landing page to generate leads is a great choice. I've outlined a few examples of these below:

Slow Communities (sometimes): First, you need to make sure you're spending enough to generate the leads you want. If you are and you still need more, then build that landing page!

Low-Performing Submarkets (sometimes): Again, make sure you're spending enough to generate those leads. It's possible that your low-performing submarkets aren't getting the funding they need to entice visitors. But if you are spending enough—build a landing page!

VIP/Coming Soon/PSWF (always): We have run landing pages specifically for "coming soon" communities and the PSWF process many times. These pages ALWAYS outperform a standard community page on the website. We see conversion rates of 10–20 percent!

Home Tours/Events (always): If the event is large enough—like a home tour—a dedicated page with event details is very effective. We typically do not have a lead-generating component on this page. Instead, we use it as an extended version of the Facebook ad. This event's landing page is also perfect for email marketing.

Quality vs. Quantity

The quality of leads from your website tends to be higher than leads from a landing page. Expect this and plan for it. How? Set the expectation up front with your sales manager and OSC. Let them know that leads from landing pages are often closer to the beginning stages of their home-buying journey. You will also want to set up a separate sales process to handle these landing-page leads if the volume overwhelms your sales team.

Remember, when the Google or Facebook user reaches your landing page, their only options are to become a lead or leave. There will always be those that submit the form without wanting to talk to anyone today or even in the near future. But by creating targeted landing pages, you increase the odds of converting that visitor.

Landing Page Template

Below you'll find a great graphic providing the elements that should be on your landing page. I'd advise you to use it as a checklist when building your first landing page.

1. **Logo:** Always include your logo on the landing page. Sometimes it may be appropriate to include the community logo as well.
2. **Phone number:** Use a tracking phone number, and you'll be surprised at the quantity of calls.
3. **Headline:** The goal of the headline is to attract and qualify. Do this by including the submarket name (city) as well as the type of home you are selling. For example: "New Homes in Tampa Bay."

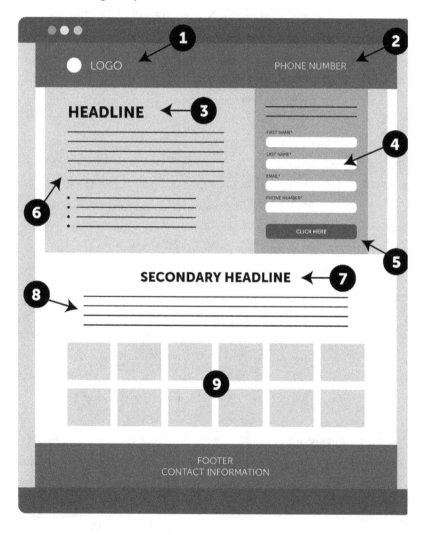

4. **Form:** Include the first name, last name, email, and phone number. Adding additional form fields almost always reduces the conversion rate. However, for some builders, this is a necessity based on lead quantity.

5. **Submit button:** Typically, using text other than "submit" converts more visitors into a lead. For example: "Become a VIP" or "View Available Homes."

6. **Supporting copy:** This section has two purposes. The first is to market the community or homes, and the second is to further qualify those who are on this page. You'll accomplish this by including pricing, floor plan information, number of bedrooms, and size of the homes.

7. **Body content headline:** The body content is an extension of the supporting copy in the above section. Use this space to talk about the community and other details that would support in convincing a web visitor to submit the form. The body content headline is a great space to position your brand or community.

8. **Body content copy:** Just like the supporting copy, use the body content to persuade web visitors to submit the form.

9. **Supporting images:** Images are very important on landing pages. Use the highest-quality and best-produced images that represent the homes you are selling. Typically, three to six images is enough to be able to give the visitor an idea of what types of homes are available.

Now What?

Generating leads doesn't have to be an uphill struggle. With a bit of planning, you can create engaging and powerful landing pages to generate new leads. By targeting specific markets and focusing on underperforming areas, you can see an increased conversion rate of visitors and gain leads.

Once you've decided to use a landing page to boost conversion rates, it's easy to create one on your own or look for a third-party tool to help. Creating specific pages for events is a great way to improve email marketing, and "coming soon" pages tend to capture a great amount of leads. If you aren't generating the leads you want, throwing money at the problem may not help. Using landing pages is a great way to reach your lead goals, increase your conversion rate, and pinpoint ways to improve your main website.

FAQS

What tools and materials are needed for the Preview Event?
Events are never easy to pull off because of the many small pieces
that go into making each one great. Here are the basics:

- Name tags for everyone on the builder/developer team and
  for prospects. Use different-colored tags to help everyone
  distinguish prospects from team members.
- Check-in form with the names of all those who have RSVP'd.
  You will not need to ask them for information a second time.
  If you have arrivals who did not RSVP, you add their information to the form at the point of check-in. When your guests
  arrive, they will feel important (you are expecting them), but
  urgency will build immediately when they see the list of
  names of others who will be attending.
- A copy of the detailed notes on each prospect from your prep
  meeting (see Markup Site Map section for more detail)
- A calendar showing the next one- to two-week period prior to
  the Grand Release, with one- to two-hour blocks for each day.
  The number-one goal of the Preview Event is to fill up these
  blocks with scheduled appointments to marry the prospect's
  previously priced-out home with the lot(s) they have interest
  in from the Preview Event. The calendar should be large and
  able to stand up for easy visibility.

- Floor plan brochures and boards to be used for easier discussion and group presentations, if needed
- Food and drink. Besides being a good host, this will give your guests something to occupy their time while they wait to "walk" home sites on paper. It will also encourage them to stay around longer, which will keep the event feeling busy.
- Gift bags. If your budget allows, consider assembling small gift bags with items from the local area or your builder. Going the extra mile here makes the story of your event more likely to spread to their friends, neighbors, and coworkers.

I've already released too much information to the public. Is it too late to try PSWF?

While it is never good to release information before the appropriate time, you can often recover from doing so. Simply remove or stop sending out the information, and proceed as normal as long as you are still sixty to ninety days away from launching.

If questioned outright by a prospect why something they saw before is now missing, you can reiterate that the goal is to only release information once it has been confirmed and is unlikely to change. The information they saw was deemed too preliminary to remain available, but you will be happy to keep them informed as updates are available. The one major hiccup in PSWF that can't be overcome is time. Simply waiting too long to begin the process or not staying organized are the more important reasons for failure, not releasing too much information.

I am planning on releasing a townhome project. Do I use the same process?

With townhome and condo projects, it is usually a good idea to reverse the release of information. This is because the variation between home sites is usually less with single-family homes due to standardization of development needed for multi-family sites.

You should release the site map (without dimensions) at the beginning and save the floor plan details for the end. Otherwise, the process is largely the same. I have seen it used successfully on both high-end infill projects and entry-level ones.

Are there other advantages to starting the process earlier, besides getting additional names for the VIP list?

Absolutely! Once your VIP list begins to reach critical mass, you have a unique opportunity, if you have the time, to gain even deeper insights into your prospects. If you are more than one hundred and twenty days away from the Preview Event, you can send out a simple survey asking questions such as:

- "What is your desired investment range?"
- "Do you need to sell your home in order to move forward?"
- "What does your ideal floor plan look like?"
- "What type of features are you expecting to be included or hoping to be able to select?"
- "What is your time frame for moving?"
- "What kind of community amenities are you hoping for?"
- "Anything else you'd like to tell us?" Include this open-ended question at the end. Just as prospects are more likely to share information with an OSC than an on-site sales rep, you'll be surprised at what they will share in a survey that they may not tell you in person.

Often, you can use the same program you use for email blasts to send out this simple survey. Successful builders find ways to incorporate what they learn from these surveys, either into the community itself or, at the very least, into their messaging.

REAL STORIES FROM THE REAL WORLD

Now you know everything you need to make PreSale Without Fail (PSWF) work for you. But usually knowing the factual information isn't the hard part. Pushing past your fears of failure after stepping out on a limb and trying something new is often much more difficult. In order to encourage you, I asked a few people in your position to share their experiences with you. These are not warm and fuzzy testimonials but real stories from the front lines—the good and the bad. I recommend that you refer back to this section at each major phase of the process in order to reaffirm your original decision to take the leap. Enjoy!

WHAT WAS THE BIGGEST ROADBLOCK OR STRUGGLE THAT YOUR TEAM HAD WHEN IMPLEMENTING PRESALE WITHOUT FAIL? WERE YOU ABLE TO SUCCESSFULLY OVERCOME IT?

One of the biggest roadblocks that we had as a company was getting the buy-in from the entire team to implement PreSale Without Fail. Some team members felt that if they didn't give potential home buyers as much information as possible immediately, they would lose the potential buyer's interest and the future sale. We successfully overcame that by testing and proving that if we control the release of community information and utilize our online sales counselors

(OSCs), we are able to have higher quality leads by launch time, equaling more sales with less hassle.

Jackie Lipinski
American Classic Homes | Seattle, WA

Withholding information until the appropriate time and denying the customer the opportunity to purchase until the Grand Release was tough at first because it took away everything we had been taught as salespeople until that point. It is very difficult to say no to qualified buyers waiving checks, saying, "I would like to buy right now." We have successfully overcome our own mental roadblock around that as we started to see the results. We have learned as a team to stay the course and get in the right mindset when opening new communities if we want to guarantee success.

Bobby Peavley
Candlelight Homes | Salt Lake City, UT

Our biggest struggle when trying to implement the PreSale Without Fail plan the first time was achieving buy-in from the online sales counselor and sales person. They were both very tentative about not releasing plans and pricing until the House in the Sky and Preview Event. They worried that we would anger the prospects and not encourage people to stay on the list until it was time to take the next step. After we did the OSC launch up until the House in the Sky phase, both the OSC and sales person realized that the program worked and that it generated more interest than previous launches and didn't anger or deter anyone.

Karen Bumgarner
Niblock Homes | Charlotte, NC

[A big roadblock for us was] getting the owner of the company and the developer to buy into the process and to stay the course. Sometimes they have personal contacts that are interested in purchasing, and they are so eager to see some return on their investment and to know that the community is going to be successful that they can't understand why they shouldn't go ahead and write a contract with the person that they have communication with. Try to get them to understand that by going through this process, instead of only having three or four sales on opening day and then having a hard time getting momentum built from there, you can probably at least double that number on opening day, and then have the momentum flow easily from there. It's hard to keep them reined in and to make sure that they trust in the process, but it's worth the effort.

Lorrie Crummie
Laurel Communities | Pittsburgh, PA

I think the very first thing is getting the whole team on the same page. The whole idea of trying something new and unknown versus the way that we've always done it before can be scary. I think everyone quickly wants to go back to what they're comfortable with and [what's] tried and true. We had everyone watch the webinars Kevin had done online, and we had also encouraged everyone to read the book. For many, watching the video was the preferred route, and then sitting down and having several meetings to flesh out what some of their concerns were. There were several lead-up meetings getting everyone's buy-in, and sometimes it felt like an uphill battle, but because I believed so strongly that we needed to do this, they saw that passion in me as well. I kept coming back and overcoming their objections on why we should try something new.

Being a custom builder, we are very anxious to always say yes and to accommodate and to move quickly—so holding back some of the information was a very foreign concept to our group. It took a lot of coaching and reminding everyone what the overall goal is and why we weren't going to go back to our old ways of always just saying "yes" or "let me price that for you" or "let me get that for you."

We were accustomed to sharing the land information first, so that was very different. Coming up with this base set of plans and customizing or doing so much planning up front kind of reversed our mentality of holding back the land. We really don't seem to build the same house twice, so really sitting down and identifying what this base set of plans needs to be, getting our estimating team to buy into pricing out all of these homes without a buyer, and getting that set up was a challenge. It was different but definitely paid off in the long run. I will say that, ironically, the very first time, one of our presale buyers ended up building our base set of plans with no changes.

I would say one of the other things was defining what success would look like for this project. Especially since it was something we had never done before.

Jenn Nowalk
Homes by Dickerson | Raleigh, NC

WHAT WAS THE THING THAT SURPRISED YOU THE MOST ABOUT HOW THE PROCESS WORKS, OR WHAT BECAME A CHALLENGE YOU COULDN'T PREDICT?

A challenge that we couldn't have predicted was that we would sell a community using the process so fast that we ended up selling our model home that we should have held onto longer to better help our next upcoming community. Not having a model home really hindered the next community launch event.

Jackie Lipinski
American Classic Homes | Seattle, WA

It sounds a little silly now, but our biggest surprise was that buyers actually waited and followed the process instead of buying from someone else. Many on the team were sure we would see more fallout.

Bobby Peavley
Candlelight Homes | Salt Lake City, UT

The amount of people that showed up for our first VIP Preview Event was very surprising. We had over sixty people show up to the event at our design center, because we did not have a model home on site, nor did we have any similar product in another neighborhood that we could invite people to. As a smaller family-owned company, that was way more than we had ever had before. At the time, the community was in a very rough stage of development, and we could not have it on site either. Those people showed up, and they were all very interested at seeing the map because that was the first time we showed the map of the community, and it was a great event that moved everyone forward.

Karen Bumgarner
Niblock Homes | Charlotte, NC

[We were surprised] how the psychology of the program had really eliminated all of the fears that buyers naturally feel when they're going through a sales process. It eliminated the fear of making a poor decision and being the only person to purchase in the beginning. It really eliminates buyer's remorse once someone goes through this whole process. I haven't had buyer's remorse from anybody that went through the process and saw that they weren't the only one and that all of these other people were interested in what they wanted. It really helps people to focus more on trying to have the opportunity to purchase what they want instead of focusing on whether they're making a "smart" decision. The psychology is really the key factor in the program, but you have to follow it to get that effect.

The thing I couldn't predict in some popular neighborhoods was having the dominating driver personality types try to push their way above the process, and to either talk to the owner directly or try to get an opportunity to write a contract ahead of time or to put more money down or to pay more to skip through the process entirely. It's important when you meet with those people to hold your ground and say that, to be fair to everybody, this is how the program works, because those people are key to creating the psychological effect for everyone else.

Lorrie Crummie
Laurel Communities | Pittsburgh, PA

The thing that surprised us the most about the process was the effect it also had on surrounding established communities. We had a close-out community nearby, and we had had a couple last remaining home sites and one inventory home there. From generating the interest around our new community with PSWF, we were actually able to close out the last three presales in that community as well as sell that inventory home. Those homes were seven hundred to a million each, so to have that as a by-product of all of our presale efforts was a huge win for us. This was especially true since the existing neighborhood had really wound down and we weren't in a model anymore. That was a huge win for us.

Jenn Nowalk
Homes by Dickerson | Raleigh, NC

WHAT WOULD YOU SAY TO SOMEONE WHO WAS NERVOUS ABOUT TRYING PRESALE WITHOUT FAIL FOR THE FIRST TIME?

It's okay to be patient when giving out community information. The most important thing you can do is control the flow of information from your company to the buyer. PreSale Without Fail helps create FOMO (fear of missing out) because when people on your interest list know they're getting the same information as other VIPs all at the same time, they're more likely to make a decision faster based off of that fear of losing out on their dream home.

Jackie Lipinski
American Classic Homes | Seattle, WA

Follow the process. Stay the course no matter how uncomfortable you feel. If done right, the score takes care of itself.

Bobby Peavley
Candlelight Homes | Salt Lake City, UT

I would say work the VIP list. Our OSC has been very complementary to the entire process, and you have to continue to work that VIP list and keep them interested. As long as you stay in front of them and you continually are sending out updates, it works. The ones who were very interested, of course, our OSC ended up knowing really well, and when it came time to start making appointments with our sales person (House in the Sky), there was no question as to who those people were.

Karen Bumgarner
Niblock Homes | Charlotte, NC

What do you have to lose? PSWF will likely double what you would have otherwise had at the initial release, and then create a stream of people that are easy to convert after that. I truly can't understand why someone wouldn't try it.

Lorrie Crummie
Laurel Communities | Pittsburgh, PA

I'd tell them obviously to do it, but you can't wing it. If you wing it, and you just kind of dip your toe in, then you'll never be successful. Going through and understanding the exact and full process is an absolute must before implementing. To do this, you have to go all in and have a very systematic, organized approach with enough team members on board and the right marketing message, and only then will you really be successful with the program.

Jenn Nowalk
Homes by Dickerson | Raleigh, NC

WHAT HAVE BEEN YOUR RESULTS FROM PRESALE WITHOUT FAIL?

After creating marketing campaigns and growing a VIP interest list for months and giving our VIPs updates about when information will be released through agents and the OSC, we launched a new twenty-home community, and after the first week of opening, we sold twelve of the twenty homes, with the homes in this community averaging around $1.3 million each.

Jackie Lipinski
American Classic Homes | Seattle, WA

We have jump-started every new community with excitement and momentum as well as a minimal fallout/cancellation rate with PreSale Without Fail. If we don't sell large numbers, we know we are maximizing profitability on each home sold. Not every community will be a home run, but when you trust the process, you know it did the best that was possible, taking all factors into consideration.

Bobby Peavley
Candlelight Homes | Salt Lake City, UT

We felt the process was very successful for our smaller-sized company. We sold over 10 percent of the community in one day—without a model home or paved streets—to an empty-nester buyer profile that typically doesn't act on faith. I don't think we could have asked for anything more, and we are excited to try the process again when we get the opportunity and see how it works the next time.

Karen Bumgarner
Niblock Homes | Charlotte, NC

My results from PreSale Without Fail have varied. In all cases, the results far surpassed what they would have been without it, but they varied by neighborhood. My best has been an opening day when we had to hold a lottery where we sold thirteen homes and then followed that with six additional homes over the next forty-five to sixty days. When you have results like that, it's so easy to keep momentum going because you're talking to new prospects with such confidence. As soon as you tell a new prospect, "We opened for sale on this day, we had to have a lottery, we've already sold thirteen houses, and the community's only been open for three weeks," that customer immediately turns back around and says, "How do I purchase?"

On the flip side, I've had neighborhoods that probably wouldn't have sold *anything* at the opening without PreSale Without Fail and would have struggled for a long time. Following the process, we were always able to get two to four sales out of the gate and build steadily from that success. In those cases, it's really important for the sales rep to be trained on how to still follow the psychology behind it all and to make the community seem successful so that you can roll on and can carry that momentum. A big part of launching a community is the sales rep's attitude and their ability to convey urgency and success even in a neighborhood that isn't as successful as they may prefer—but is still beyond what the market would lead ownership to expect.

Lorrie Crummie
Laurel Communities | Pittsburgh, PA

We ended up getting four presales in our new community at an average price point over $700K. That equals around 22 percent of the community in one day. We also had the three presales in an older close-out community just up the street. Those homes were $800K–$1 million. We also sold an inventory home there to close out the community completely! All in all, for us, it was a complete win and worth every ounce of effort that we put into planning it.

Jenn Nowalk
Homes by Dickerson | Raleigh, NC

ABOUT THE AUTHOR

Kevin Oakley has over fifteen years of experience running marketing and sales operations for home builders of all shapes, sizes, and areas of expertise. Kevin has worked for two different multibillion-dollar revenue builders (NVR and Maronda Homes) and for a private family-owned builder (Heartland Homes). In 2018, he was also named to *Professional Builder* magazine's "40 Under 40" list for his leadership and contribution to the industry at large.

During his two years with NVR, a top-five home builder, Kevin had full responsibility for all aspects of two home-building divisions in the Pittsburgh MSA, with revenues over $125 million. While at Heartland Homes, Kevin's management helped to grow sales by 15–20 percent each year during the downturn from 2008 to 2012, while simultaneously shrinking the marketing budget by over $1.5 million dollars.

Kevin's extensive background and time spent in the trenches allows him to uniquely connect with the challenges you face in any real estate market. Whether it's launching new communities, increasing online lead volume or conversion, improving your customer's experience, lowering marketing costs, helping with web design, and so much more, he has a strategy for success. Kevin speaks regularly at the International Builder's Show and Pacific Coast Builder's Conference, as well as select local home-building associations and home-building companies looking to gain an edge over the competition. He is also the co-host (along with Andrew Peek) of the Market Proof Marketing podcast (www.MarketProofMarketing.com), the industry leading weekly show for the latest digital marketing insights and special guest interviews.

You can reach Kevin at Kevin@DoYouConvert.com.

CPSIA information can be obtained
at www.ICGtesting.com
Printed in the USA
LVHW08s1017010918
588804LV00022B/96/P

9 781610 660716